STATISTICAL HISTORY

OF

BENEVOLENT CONTRIBUTIONS

IN THE

PAST SIXTEEN YEARS.

FOR THE USE OF THE

American Board of Commissioners for Foreign Missions,

SEPTEMBER, 1852.

PREPARED BY ONE OF THE SECRETARIES.

SECOND EDITION, REVISED SEPTEMBER, 1853.

BOSTON:
PRESS OF T. R. MARVIN, 42 CONGRESS STREET.
1853.

STATISTICAL HISTORY

OF

BENEVOLENT CONTRIBUTIONS

IN THE

PAST SIXTEEN YEARS.

Are Foreign and Home Missions advancing in this country?

Some have supposed, that the receipts of the American Board of Commissioners for Foreign Missions have been stationary, the past ten years. Has it been so, on the whole?

The Missionary Spirit first put itself forth effectively in *Foreign* Missions, and the tide of contributions seemed, for a time, to flow chiefly in that direction. Do our *Home* Missions now receive a fair proportionate support?

These, with other kindred inquiries, can be answered only by means of statistical investigations. To furnish the facts for a *full* and *perfect* reply to the third of the above inquiries, would require the investigation to be pushed farther than comports with our time, if not with our sources of information. Such an extended inquiry, however, is not needful to the object we have in view, as will appear in the sequel.

It is not an easy matter, in respect to *all* the Societies that are to pass under review, to say precisely what have been their annual receipts during every one of the past sixteen or twenty years; nor is it quite possible to say, in respect to some of them, what portion of their outlay is properly chargeable to foreign objects, and what to home objects. Where there was no way but to conjecture, we have done the best we could. In stating the receipts of one of the Societies, it has been necessary, for obvious reasons, to deduct the grants of our National Government and of Bible and Tract Societies. In one instance we found, that the table we had compiled from the treasurer's accounts did not, for some reason, correspond exactly with a list of receipts for a course of years we subsequently found in the body of one of the Annual Reports. It seemed proper to correct our table by the Report.

It may perhaps be possible to detect not a few errors in the tables; though not enough, it is believed, even in the aggregate, to affect the value of the results. There may be errors of judgment, in determining what were the actual receipts to be reckoned in such an investigation; errors in the transfer of numbers to paper; errors in copying; errors in the arithmetical calculations; and some errors in the press. The author of these tables could not give himself exclusively to the business, except in numerous short portions of time. They were a small part of his share in the laborious preparation incumbent on the Secretaries of the Board for the Annual Meeting. Should others be incited to revise these tables, and do the work more effectively, he will still feel that his labor has not been in vain.

The object of the investigation—what in fact impelled to it—not only did not require that contributions from Religious Denominations with which the American Board has no immediate connection, should be reckoned, but it required that they should not be reckoned. The object was, to ascertain wherefore the receipts of the Board have increased no faster during the last ten or twelve years, and what is the prospect in future. The careful and reflecting observer will be able to see that, whatever the retarding influences were, they are not such as bear unfavorably on the present prospects of Missions, whether Foreign or Domestic.

FOREIGN MISSIONS.

American Board of Commissioners for Foreign Missions.

I. *Receipts of the Board.*

The receipts of each year are given; the receipts in each period of four years; the increase in those periods respectively; the average annual receipts for each of the periods; and the increase (decrease in one instance) in the average annual receipts of each period.

Years.	Periods.	Receipts.	Periods of 4 years.	Increase.	Av. Ann. Receipts.	Increase.
1811,		$999 52				
1812,		13,611 50				
1813,		11,361 18				
1814,		12,265 56				
1815,		9,493 89				
	1.		$46,732 13		11,683	10,684
1816,		12,501 03				
1817,		29,948 63				
1818,		34,727 72				
1819,		37,520 63				
	2.		114,698 01	67,966	28,674	16,991
1820,		39,949 45				
1821,		46,354 95				
1822,		60,087 87				
1823,		55,758 94				
	3.		202,151 21	87,413	50,537	21,863
1824,		47,483 58				
1825,		55,716 18				
1826,		61,616 25				
1827,		88,341 89				
	4.		253,157 90	51,006	63,289	12,752
1828,		102,009 64				
1829,		106,928 26				
1830,		83,019 37				
1831,		100,934 09				
	5.		392,891 36	39,734	98,222	34,933
1832,		130,574 12				
1833,		145,847 77				
1834,		152,386 10				
1835,		163,340 19				
	6.		592,148 18	199,257	148,037	49,815
1836,		176,232 15				
1837,		252,076 55				
1838,		236,170 98				
1839,		244,169 82				
	7.		908,649 50	316,501	227,162	79,125
1840,		241,691 04				
1841,		235,189 30				
1842,		318,396 53				
1843,		244,254 43				
	8.		1,039,531 30	130,882	259,882	32,720
1844,		236,394 37				
1845,		255,112 96				
1846,		262,073 55				
1847,		211,402 76				
	9.		964,983 64	*74,547	241,245	*18,637
1848,		254,056 46				
1849,		291,705 27				
1850,		251,862 28				
1851,		274,902 21				
	10.		1,072,526 22	107,543	268,131	26,886
1852,		301,732 70				
1853,		314,922 88				

* Less than in the preceding period.

II. *Expenditures of the Board.*

Year.	Periods.	Expenditures.	Periods.	Increase.	Av. Ann. Expenditure.	Increase.
1811,						
1812,		$9,699				
1813,		8,611				
1814,		7,078				
1815,		5,027				
	1.		$30,415		7,603	
1816,		15,934				
1817,		20,485				
1818,		36,346				
1819,		40,337				
	2.		113,102	82,687	28,275	20,672
1820,		57,621				
1821,		46,771				
1822,		60,474				
1823,		66,380				
	3.		231,246	118,144	57,811	29,536
1824,		54,157				
1825,		41,469				
1826,		59,012				
1827,		103,430				
	4.		258,068	26,822	64,517	6,706
1828,		107,676				
1829,		92,533				
1830,		84,798				
1831,		98,313				
	5.		383,320	125,252	95,830	31,313
1832,		120,954				
1833,		149,906				
1834,		159,779				
1835,		163,254				
	6.		593,893	210,573	148,473	117,160
1836,		210,407				
1837,		254,589				
1838,		230,642				
1839,		227,491				
	7.		923,129	329,236	230,782	82,309
1840,		246,601				
1841,		268,914				
1842,		261,147				
1843,		256,687				
	8.		1,033,349	110,220	258,337	27,555
1844,		244,371				
1845,		216,817				
1846,		257,605				
1847,		264,783				
	9.		983,576	*49,773	245,894	*12,443
1848,		282,330				
1849,		263,418				
1850,		254,329				
1851,		284,830				
	10.		1,084,907	101,331	271,256	25,362
1852,		257,727				
1853,		310,607				

* Less than in the preceding period.

III. *Comparative View of the Board's Receipts and Expenditures.*

Periods.	Receipts.	Expenditures.	Excess.
1811,	$999		*999
1812—15,	46,732	30,415	*16,317
1816—19,	114,698	113,102	*1,596
1820—23,	202,151	231,246	29,095
1824—27,	253,157	258,068	4,911
1828—31,	392,891	383,320	*9,571
1832—35,	592,148	593,893	1,745
1836—39,	908,649	923,129	14,480
1840—43,	1,039,531	1,033,349	*6,182
1844—47,	964,983	983,576	18,593
1848—51,	1,072,526	1,084,907	12,381
Total,	$5,588,465	$5,635,005	$81,205
* Excess of Receipts, ...			34,655
Excess of Expenditures in forty years, . .			$46,540

IV. *Receipts of the Board from Massachusetts, Connecticut, and New York, derived from the supplementary statement to the Treasurer's Accounts.*

(Only what came through Auxiliaries.)

Year.	Massachusetts.	Connecticut.	New York.
1832,	$26,007	16,930	18,255
1833,	25,487	17,203	25,844
1834,	28,511	17,398	22,388
1835,	28,685	17,509	24,559
1836,	28,154	19,445	24,983
1837,	37,541	28,119	37,385
1838,	38,213	38,526	30,610
1839,	33,113	31,730	32,969
1840,	53,847	34,724	28,613
1841,	53,838	33,359	32,298
1842,	71,106	42,806	35,812
1843,	59,546	35,076	30,874
1844,	59,854	30,504	28,354
1845,	64,635	33,227	29,555
1846,	52,548	29,379	22,493
1847,	52,421	27,370	27,596
(The whole amount of donations.)			
1848,	71,459	39,488	*53,703
1849,	91,874	42,294	70,534
1850,	76,069	39,630	50,569
1851,	77,280	38,534	60,800

SUMMARY.

Periods.	Massachusetts.	Connecticut.	New York.
1832—35,	$108,690	69,040	91,036
1836—39,	137,021	117,920	125,947
1840—43,	238,347	145,965	127,527
1844—47,	269,458	121,480	107,998
1848—51,	316,682	159,946	*235,606
Total,	1,070,198	614,351	688,114
	Increase.		
Period 2*d*,	$28,331	48,880	34,911
" 3*d*,	101,326	28,045	1,580
" 4*th*,	31,111	†24,485	†19,529
" 5*th*,	47,224	38,466	*127,608

* A considerable portion of the receipts from New York State do not come through Auxiliaries.
† Less than in the preceding period.

V. *Receipts of the Board from the Western States, in each of the last four years.*

Year.	Ohio.	Indiana.	Illinois.	Michigan.	Wisconsin.	Iowa.	Missouri.	Ark.	Kentucky.	Tenn.
1848,	10,562	1,030	3,265	3,290	808	161	1,112	65	259	1,266
1849,	10,718	1,910	3,205	2,632	1,066	375	811		84	884
1850,	11,393	1,404	2,767	2,300	703	217	846		124	1,035
1851,	11,905	1,961	3,591	2,119	927	331	303		127	641
Total,	44,578	6,305	12,828	10,341	3,504	1,084	3,072	65	594	3,826

VI. *Increase of the Receipts of the Board from New England and New York, in the last twenty years.*

Certain Districts are selected, in each of the States, which may serve as the basis of the rate of increase on the whole. Of course it will be only an approximation.

Year.	Cumberland Co., Me.	Hillsboro' Co., N. H.	Rutland Co., Vt.	Berkshire Co., Ms.
1832,	$943	1,847	936	1,967
1833,	1,226	1,783	743	1,970
1834,	1,232	1,759	828	1,667
1835,	1,242	1,856	612	1,612
	———4,643	———7,245	———3,119	———7,216
1836,	769	1,699	721	1,691
1837,	2,068	1,991	1,519	1,404
1838,	2,289	2,167	1,366	1,833
1839,	2,211	2,129	1,350	2,317
	———7,337	———7,986	———4,956	———7,245
1840,	2,715	2,788	1,754	1,009
1841,	2,072	3,038	1,915	4,758
1842,	4,016	3,416	2,781	2,879
1843,	1,813	2,882	1,545	2,220
	———10,616	———12,124	———7,995	———10,866
1844,	2,129	2,971	1,607	3,121
1845,	2,177	2,792	1,650	2,621
1846,	2,013	2,144	1,501	2,072
1847,	1,893	2,195	1,378	2,523
	———8,212	———10,102	———6,136	———10,337
1848	2,491	2,366	1,697	3,829
1849,	1,935	3,223	1,513	2,275
1850,	2,507	2,644	1,690	2,990
1851,	2,382	2,295	1,346	2,595
	———9,315	———10,528	———6,246	———11,689

Year.	Brookfield Asso., Ms.	Worc'r Central, Ms.	Boston, Ms.	Hartford Co., Ct.	Windham Co., Ct.
1832,	$1,298	1,761	7,446	3,807	1,143
1833,	1,382	1,814	8,141	4,649	1,074
1834,	1,578	2,023	9,338	4,175	1,171
1835,	1,461	2,081	8,611	4,293	1,061
	——5,719	——7,679	——33,536	——16,924	——4,449
1836,	1,530	2,055	8,343	3,940	1,357
1837,	2,433	3,192	13,129	6,316	1,471
1838,	2,711	4,275	8,842	11,882	2,208
1839,	2,762	3,576	7,571	8,156	2,562
	——9,436	——13,098	——37,885	——30,294	——7,598
1840,	2,619	4,816	12,179	7,056	2,393
1841,	2,759	3,927	14,143	8,877	2,737
1842,	2,884	5,588	18,479	9,284	3,449
1843,	2,557	4,480	16,921	9,389	2,622
	——10,819	——18,811	——61,722	——34,606	——11,201
1844,	3,298	4,148	15,630	5,934	2,464
1845,	4,004	7,599	15,393	7,105	2,533
1846,	3,164	4,155	14,105	6,727	2,264
1847,	2,718	4,120	15,913	5,771	2,166
	——13,184	——20,022	——61,041	——25,537	——9,427
1848,	3,302	4,464	13,795	7,587	2,525
1849,	3,245	5,584	22,122	9,252	2,932
1850,	4,295	5,127	17,537	6,234	2,105
1851,	3,486	4,618	19,127	6,743	2,167
	——14,328	——19,793	——72,581	——29,816	——9,729

Year.	N. Y. City & Brooklyn.	Geneva & Vic. N. Y.	Monroe Co. N. Y.	Oneida Co. N. Y.	Buffalo and Vic.
1832,	$9,984		2,025	4,211	
1833,	14,044		1,640	5,498	
1834,	7,637		2,685	3,710	
1835,	13,401		1,876	4,537	
	——45,066		——8,226	——17,956	
1836,	12,164	2,147	3,269	2,724	
1837,	17,107	4,911	3,915	4,282	542
1838,	11,234	7,693	3,453	3,123	338
1839,	13,769	8,531	3,301	2,956	690
	——54,274	——23,282	——14,938	——13,085	——1,570
1840,	11,132	6,719	2,978	2,899	501
1841,	12,447	9,337	2,509	2,935	972
1842,	15,301	7,942	2,999	2,226	1,402
1843,	13,390	7,172	3,858	2,042	678
	——52,270	——31,170	——12,344	——10,102	——3,553
1844,	10,923	6,428	3,608	1,778	1,306
1845,	11,885	6,167	3,373	2,112	787
1846,	7,974	4,977	1,960	1,776	1,063
1847,	13,807	4,251	3,196	1,895	762
	——44,589	——21,803	——12,137	——7,561	——3,918
1848,	11,598	4,557	3,944	1,818	1,523
1849,	21,252	5,204	4,113	2,376	1,363
1850,	13,241	5,229	1,976	1,457	809
1851,	17,847	6,262	4,873	1,555	1,846
	——63,938	——21,252	——14,906	——7,206	——5,541

The following is a Summary View.

1. In New England.

	First Period.	Last Period.	Increase.
Boston, Ms.	$33,536	72,581	39,045
Worcester Central, Ms.	7,679	19,793	12,114
Brookfield Association, Ms.	5,719	14,328	8,609
Berkshire Co., Ms.	7,216	11,689	4,473
Hartford Co., Ct.	16,924	29,816	12,892
Windham Co., Ct.	4,449	9,729	5,280
Rutland, Vt.	3,119	6,246	3,127

Hillsboro', N. H.	7,245	10,528	3,283
Cumberland, Me.	4,643	9,315	4,672
	90,530	184,025	93,495

2. In New York.

	First.	Fifth.	Increase.
N. Y. City and Brooklyn,	$45,066	63,938	18,872
Geneva and Vicinity,	23,282	21,252	*2,030
Monroe Co.	8,226	14,906	6,680
Oneida Co.	17,956	7,206	*10,750
Buffalo and Vicinity,	3,553	5,541	1,988
	98,083	112,843	14,760

* Decrease.

VII. *Donations from States to the Board, in the years* 1839, 1844, *and* 1851.

The donations for 1839 and 1844, are taken from tables compiled and printed in pamphlet form several years ago. Those for 1851, are from the table supplementary to the Treasurer's Accounts in the Report for that year.

States.	1839.	1844.	1851.
Maine,	$6,279	7,822	7,122
New Hampshire,	9,151	10,052	10,891
Vermont,	9,142	10,022	8,515
Massachusetts,	48,876	73,369	77,280
Connecticut,	33,975	37,259	38,534
Rhode Island,	1,652	2,957	2,678
New York,	48,554	45,828	60,800
New Jersey,	5,180	6,486	9,716
Pennsylvania,	12,823	10,558	12,466
Delaware,	515	607	540
Maryland,	1,272	768	2,152
District of Columbia,	631	646	642
Virginia,	392	2,444	1,400
North Carolina,	157	22	48
South Carolina,	1,303	1,139	1,239
Georgia,	2,459	1,770	3,395
Florida,	35	20	
Alabama,	1,399	843	244
Mississippi,	84	191	105
Louisiana,	130	281	185
Tennessee,	1,462	1,980	641
Kentucky,	855	482	127
Arkansas,	70	441	
Missouri,	1,438	475	303
Iowa, Wisconsin,	10	241	
Iowa,			331
Wisconsin,			927
Illinois,	2,240	1,948	3,591
Indiana,	690	928	1,961
Michigan,	318	1,263	2,119
Ohio,	7,628	9,874	11,905
Canada,		914	
Foreign Countries,	2,671	2,204	12,384
Co-operating Societies,	12,549		
Unknown,	685		
Texas,			36
California,			120
Minesota Territory,			104
Oregon Territory,			177

Other Societies operating in Foreign Missions.

VIII. *Receipts of the General Assembly's Board of Foreign Missions.*

Year.	Receipts.	Periods.	Average Annual Receipts.
1838,	$44,748		
1839,	56,150		
		*100,898	50,449
1840,	54,425		
1841,	62,344		
1842,	58,924		
1843,	54,760		
		230,453	57,613
1844,	66,674		
1845,	72,117		
1846,	76,395		
1847,	82,739		
		297,925	74,481
1848,	89,165		
1849,	96,294		
1850,	104,665		
1851,	108,544		
		398,668	99,667
1852,	117,882		
1853,	122,615		

The grants of Bible and Tract Societies, and appropriations from the United States Government for Indian missions, have been deducted.

* For two years only.

IX. *Receipts of the American Bible Society as the result of Donations, and the appropriations made of the same.*

Year.	Receipts.	Periods.	Dona. for For. Dis.	App. for For. Uses.	Periods.	For Home Uses.
1832,	$47,564			631		
1833,	46,091			15,300		
1834,	54,570			17,000		
1835,	62,868			35,500		
		211,093			68,431	142,662
1836,	58,781		13,789	39,070		
1837,	35,728		6,589	6,326		
1838,	44,365		3,631	20,230		
1839,	53,285		5,840	19,465		
		192,159			85,091	107,068
1840,	48,030		6,418	10,549		
1841,	61,840		2,686	30,794		
1842,	74,530		3,843	16,619		
1843,	65,244		2,419	15,518		
		249,644			73,480	176,164
1844,	67,606		1,247	23,945		
1845,	68,468		1,091	13,792		
1846,	104,551		1,526	1,500		
1847,	73,946		965	18,000		
		314,571			57,237	257,334
1848,	94,505		1,938	9,500		
1849,	91,804		10,762	11,188		
1850,	117,794		1,483	17,900		
1851,	120,065			9,100		
		424,168			47,788	376,380
1852,		1,391,635			332,027	1,059,609

X. *Receipts of the American Tract Society as the result of Donations, and the appropriations made of the same.*

Year.	Receipts.	Periods.	App. For. Dis.	Periods.	Colportage.	Periods.	Home Uses.	Dona. For. Dis.
1832,	$24,476		5,044					
1833,	31,229		10,000					
1834,	35,213		20,000					
1835,	60,628	—151,546	30,000	—65,044			86,502	
1836,	56,638		35,000					29,949
1837,	72,933		35,000					31,332
1838,	37,175		10,000					11,985
1839,	55,854	—222,600	30,000	—110,000			112,600	28,099
1840,	41,476		20,000					19,594
1841,	41,752		25,000					23,390
1842,	34,942		15,000					11,845
1843,	46,326	—164,496	15,000	—75,000	5,929	—5,929	89,506	5,929
1844,	56,680		20,000		15,011			4,382
1845,	66,080		6,000		25,382			1,313
1846,	71,132		15,000		31,043			4,305
1847,	67,771	—261,663	10,000	—51,000	40,191	—111,627	210,663	2,308
1848,	105,915		11,000		50,559			1,729
1849,	94,081		14,000		58,106			2,091
1850,	105,894		15,000		66,274			1,812
1851,	109,897	—415,787	20,000	—60,000	73,278	—248,217	355,787	790
1852,	116,406		20,000		79,073			
1853,	147,374							
		1,216,092		361,044		365,773	855,058	

XI. *Receipts of the American Protestant Society, the Foreign Evangelical Society, and the American and Foreign Christian Union.*

American Protestant Society.

Year.	Receipts.	Periods.	Average Annual Receipts.
1844,	$6,746		
1845,	9,184		
1846,	19,709		
1847,	25,028	—60,667	15,166
1848,	28,704		
1849,	29,137	—57,841	28,920

Foreign Evangelical Society.

Year.	Receipts.	Periods.	Average Annual Receipts.
1840,	$10,210		
1841,	14,357		
1842,	10,900		
1843,	10,766	—46,233	11,558
1844,	13,356		
1845,	16,249		
1846,	20,146		
1847,	14,855	—64,606	16,151
1848,	19,439		
1849,	24,484		

* American and Foreign Christian Union.

Year.	Receipts.	Periods.	Av. Ann. Receipts.	App. to Home Uses.
1850,	$57,223			
1851,	56,265	—157,411	39,352	†64,000

* Constituted by the union of the Foreign Evangelical Society, the American Protestant Society, and the Christian Alliance.

† Conjectural.

XII. *Receipts of the American Missionary Association.*

Year.	Receipts.	Periods.	Av. Ann. Rec.	App. to Home Missions.	
1847,	$13,033				
1848,	17,095				
1849,	21,982			1,581	
1850,	25,159			3,186	
1851,	34,535			2,632	
		98,771	24,692		7,399

XIII. *Receipts for Foreign Missions, in Periods of four years each.*

Periods.	Amer. Board of Com. for For. Missions.	Pres. Board of For. Missions.	Amer. Bible Society.	Amer. Tract Society.	Am. & For. Ch. Union.	Am. Miss. Asso'n.
1836—39,	$908,649	*100,898	†85,091	†110,000		
1840—43,	1,039,531	230,453	73,480	75,000	46,233	
1844—47,	964,983	297,925	57,237	51,000	64,606	
1848—51,	1,072,526	398,668	47,788	60,000	93,411	91,372
	3,985,689	1,027,944	263,596	296,000	204,250	91,372

3,985,689
1,027,944
263,596
296,000
204,250
91,372—$5,868,851, total in 16 years for Foreign Missions.

* Two years only. † Appropriations by the Society.

XIV. *Growth o the Foreign Missions.*

Periods.	Society.	Receipts in Periods.	Total of Receipts in the Periods.	Average Annual Receipts.	
1836—39,	Am. Board Com. For. Miss.	$908,649		227,162	
[1838, 9]	Pres. Board For. Miss.	100,898		25,224	
	Amer. Bible Society,	85,091		21,272	
	Amer. Tract Society,	110,000		27,500	
			1,204,638		301,159
1840—43,	Am. Board Com. For. Miss.	1,039,531		259,882	
	Pres. Board For. Miss.	230,453		57,613	
	Amer. Bible Society,	73,480		18,370	
	Amer. Tract Society,	75,000		18,750	
	For. Evangelical Society,	46,238		11,559	
			1,464,702		366,175
1844—47,	Am. Board Com. For. Miss.	964,983		241,245	
	Pres. Board For. Miss.	297,925		74,481	
	Amer. Bible Society,	57,237		14,309	
	Amer. Tract Society,	51,000		12,750	
	For. Evangelical Society,	64,606		16,151	
			1,435,751		358,937
1848—51,	Am. Board Com. For. Miss.	1,072,526		268,131	
	Pres. Board For. Miss.	398,668		99,667	
	Amer. Bible Society,	47,788		11,947	
	Amer. Tract Society,	60,000		15,000	
	Am. and For. Chr. Union,	93,411		23,352	
	Am. Miss. Association,	91,372		22,843	
			1,763,765		440,941

HOME MISSIONS.

XV. *Receipts of the American Home Missionary Society.*

Society's Year.	Receipts.	Periods of Four Years.	Inc. in the Periods.	Av. Ann. Receipts.
1—1826-27,	$18,140 76			
2—1827-28,	20,035 78			
3—1828-29,	26,997 31			
4—1829-30,	33,929 44			
5—1830-31,	48,124 73	129,087		32,271
6—1831-32,	49,422 12			
7—1832-33,	68,627 17			
8—1833-34,	78,911 44			
9—1834-35,	88,863 22	285,823	156,737	71,455
10—1835-36,	101,565 15			
11—1836-37,	85,701 59			
12—1837-38,	86,522 45			
13—1838-39,	82,564 63	356,353	70,530	89,088
14—1839-40,	78,345 20			
15—1840-41,	85,413 34			
16—1841-42,	92,463 64			
17—1842-43,	99,812 24	356,034	*319	89,008
18—1843-44,	101,904 99			
19—1844-45,	121,946 28			
20—1845-46,	125,124 70			
21—1846-47,	116,617 94	465,593	109,559	116,398
22—1847-48,	140,197 10			
23—1848-49,	145,925 91			
24—1849-50,	157,160 78			
25—1850-51,	150,942 25	594,226	128,630	148,556
26—1851-52,	160,062 25			
27—1852-53,	171,734 24			

* Less than in the preceding period.

XVI. *Receipts of the Presbyterian Board of Home Missions.*

Year.	Receipts.	Periods.	Increase.	Av. Ann. Receipts.
1832,	$23,030			
1833,	27,058			
1834,	23,451			
1835,	22,664	96,203		24,050
1836,	25,000			
1837,	30,961			
1838,	22,747			
1839,	24,063	102,771	6,568	25,692
1840,	21,413			
1841,	20,636			
1842,	16,321			
1843,	19,108	77,478	*25,293	19,369
1844,	23,013			
1845,	29,688			
1846,	32,322			
1847,	30,870	115,893	38,415	28,973
1848,	33,390			
1849,	44,432			
1850,	79,043			
1851,	82,818	239,683	123,790	59,920

* Less than in the preceding period.

[NOTE.—The preceding abstract of the receipts of the Presbyterian Board of Home Missions, was prepared from the Annual Reports of that Board. Subsequently to the publication of this pamphlet, the following official list of receipts in the above years appeared in the "Home Record;" including not only the receipts at Philadelphia, but also those of the local agencies at Louisville, Pittsburg, and the Synod of Ohio.

1832,	$20,692 10	1838,	34,238 14	1844,	36,595 38	1850,	67,654 19
1833,	21,471 29	1839,	39,419 63	1845,	45,821 15	1851,	74,974 27
1834,	24,029 05	1840,	39,225 90	1846,	47,631 98	1852, eleven	
1835,	22,135 93	1841,	33,522 43	1847,	51,809 77	months,	64,356 29
1836,	30,040 80	1842,	32,082 24	1848,	56,147 80		
1837,	29,715 73	1843,	29,934 52	1849,	70,440 37		$871,938 96]

☞ For Receipts of *American Bible Society; American Tract Society; American Protestant, Foreign Evangelical,* and *Foreign Christian Union,* and *American Missionary Association,* see ix, x, xi, xii, pp. 11—13; numbered, in first edition, xvii—xx.

XXI. *Receipts of the Society for the Promotion of Collegiate and Theological Education at the West.*

Year.	Receipts.	Periods.	Year.	Receipts.	Periods.
1844,	$17,004		1848,	$12,339	
1845,	10,967		1849,	11,001	
1846,	15,686		1850,	17,623	
1847,	14,113	—57,770	1851,	16,962	—57,925

A much larger sum than this was actually given for the Colleges in this space of time, though not through this Society.

XXII. *Receipts of the American Sunday School Union as the result of Donations.*

Year.	Receipts.	Periods.	Average Annual Receipts.
1832,	$34,691		
1833,	19,711		
1834,	28,611		
1835,	26,988	—110,001	27,500
1836,	38,321		
1837,	34,035		
1838,	22,423		
1839,	15,384	—110,163	27,540
1840,	14,134		
1841,	14,259		
1842,	14,844		
1843,	12,311	—55,548	13,887
1844,	14,343		
1845,	25,369		
1846,	25,019		
1847,	22,777	—87,508	21,877
1848,	31,092		
1849,	31,189		
1850,	35,533		
1851,	34,807	—132,621	33,155
1852,	50,038		

XXIII. *Receipts of the American Education Society.*

Year.	Receipts.	Periods.	Average Annual Receipts.
1832,	$42,030		
1833,	47,836		
1834,	57,818		
1835,	83,062	230,746	57,686
1836,	63,227		
1837,	65,574		
1838,	55,660		
1839,	55,075	239,536	59,884
1840,	51,963		
1841,	63,113		
1842,	34,491		
1843,	33,789	183,356	45,839
1844,	34,811		
1845,	34,842		
1846,	39,348		
1847,	28,299	137,300	34,325
1848,	24,974		
1849,	27,301		
1850,	28,428		
1851,	27,591	108,294	27,073
1852,	29,376		
1853,	22,729		

XXIV. *Presbyterian Board of Education.*

Year.	Receipts.	Periods.	Average Annual Receipts.
1832,			
1833,			
1834,	$44,585		
1835,	37,038	*81,623	20,405
1836,	50,064		
1837,	41,850		
1838,	33,094		
1839,	33,562	158,570	39,642
1840,	23,273		
1841,	†24,000		
1842,	24,538		
1843,	29,104	100,915	25,228
1844,	31,057		
1845,	31,723		
1846,	34,953		
1847,	†34,000	131,733	32,933
1848,	31,078		
1849,	37,754		
1850,	32,447		
1851,	36,501	137,780	34,445

* For two years only.

† Conjectural.

XXV. *Receipts for Home Missions, in Periods of four years each.*

Periods.	Amer. Home Miss. Society.	Pres. Board of Home Missions.	Amer. Bible Society.	Amer. Tract Society.	Am. Prot. Soc. & A. & F. Ch. Un.
1832—35,	$285,823	96,203	142,662	86.502	
1836—39,	356 353	102 771	107,068	112 600	
1840—43,	356,034	77,478	176,164	89,506	
1844—47,	465,593	115,893	257,334	210,663	60,667
1848—51,	594,226	239,683	376,380	355,787	121,841
	$2,058,029	632,028	1,059,608	855,058	182,508

Periods.	Western Coll. Society.	Am. Miss. Assoc.	Am. Sun. Sch. Union.	Am. Educa. Society.	Pres. Board of Educ.
1832—35,			110,001	230,746	81,623
1836—39,			110,163	239,536	158,570
1840—43,			55,548	183,356	100,915
1844—47,	57,770		87,508	137,300	131,733
1848—51,	57,925	7,399	132,621	108,294	137,780
	115,695	7,399	495,841	899,232	610,621

610,621
899,232
495,841
7,399
115,695
182,508
855,058
1,059,608
632,028
2,058,029
$6,916,019

Period, 1832—35, ...	$285,823	
	96,203	
	142,662	
	86,502	
	110,001	
	230,746	
	81,623	
		1,033,560
In 16 years for Home Missions, ...		$5,882,459

XXVI. *Growth of the Home Missions.*

Periods.	Society.	Receipts in Periods.	Totals of Receipts in the Periods.	Average Annual Receipts.	
1836-39,	Amer. Home Miss. Society,	$356,353		89,088	
	Pres. Board Home Missions,	102,771		25,692	
	American Bible Society,	107,068		26,767	
	American Tract Society,	112,600		28,150	
	American Education Society,	239,536		59,884	
	American Sunday School Union,	110,163		27,540	
	Presbyterian Board Education,	158,570		39,642	
			1,187,061		$296,765

Periods.	Society.	Receipts in Periods.	Totals of Receipts in the Periods.	Average Annual Receipts.	
1840-43,	Amer. Home Miss. Society,	$356,034		89,008	
	Pres. Board Home Missions,	77,478		19,369	
	American Bible Society,	176,164		44,041	
	American Tract Society,	89,506		22,376	
	American Education Society,	183,356		45,839	
	American Sunday School Union,	55,548		13,887	
	Presbyterian Board Education,	100,915		25,228	
		———	1,039,001	———	259,750
1844-47,	Amer. Home Miss. Society,	465,593		116,398	
	Pres. Board Home Missions,	115,893		28,973	
	American Bible Society,	257,334		64,333	
	American Tract Society,	210,663		52,665	
	American Education Society,	137,300		34,325	
	American Sunday School Union,	87,508		21,877	
	American Protestant Society,	60,667		15,166	
	Western College Society,	57,770		14,442	
	Presbyterian Board Education,	131,733		32,933	
		———	1,524,461	———	381,115
1848-51,	Amer. Home Miss. Society,	594,226		148,556	
	Pres. Board Home Missions,	239,683		59,920	
	American Bible Society,	376,380		94,096	
	American Tract Society,	355,787		88,946	
	American Education Society,	108,294		27,073	
	American Sunday School Union,	132,621		33,155	
	American Protestant Society and Am. and For. Christian Union,	121,841		30,460	
	Western College Society,	57,925		14,481	
	American Missionary Association,	7,399		1,849	
	Presbyterian Board Education,	137,780		34,445	
		———	2,131,936	———	532,984

Annual Average Receipts for each Period.

Periods.	American Home Miss. Society.	Presbyterian Board of Home Miss.	American Bible Society.	American Tract Society.	American Education Society.	Presbyterian Board of Education.	American Sunday Sch. Union.	Western College Society.
1836-39,	$89,088	25,692	26,767	28,150	59,884	39,642	27,540	
1840-43,	89,008	19,369	44,041	22,376	45,839	25,228	13,887	
1844-47,	116,398	28,973	64,333	52,665	34,325	32,933	21,877	14,442
1848-51,	148,556	59,920	94,095	88,946	27,073	34,445	33,155	14,481

XXVII. *Growth of Foreign and Home Missions.*

	FOREIGN MISSIONS.		HOME MISSIONS.	
	Totals.	Average annual.	Totals.	Average annual.
1836—39,	$1,204,638	301,159	1,187,061	296,765
1840—43,	1,464,702	366,175	1,039,001	259,750
1844—47,	1,435,751	358,937	1,524,461	381,112
1848—51,	1,763,765	440,941	2,131,936	532,984
Total,	$5,868,856	1,467,212	5,882,456	1,470,611
Average,	$1,467,214	366,803	1,470,614	367,652
1848—51,	1,763,765	440,941	2,131,936	532,984
1836—39,	1,204,638	301,159	1,187,061	296,765
Increase,	$559,127	139,782	944,875	236,219

ENGLISH FOREIGN MISSIONS.

The means are at hand for stating the receipts of English Foreign Missionary Societies, to a great extent, but not of those operating in the Home Missionary department. It will be sufficient, however, to give the receipts of two of the larger Missionary Societies, occupying the same ground, as regards the popular mind, with the larger benevolent societies generally in this country.

XXVIII. *Receipts of the London Missionary Society.*

Year.	Receipts.	Periods.	Average Annual Receipts.
1836,	£63,714		
1837,	71,335		
1838,	84.821		
1839,	80,321	—300,191	£75,047
1840,	94,954		
1841,	96,771		
1842,	91,795		
1843,	93,947	—377,467	94,366
1844,	89,124		
1845,	90.715		
1846,	82,991		
1847,	81,183	—344,013	86,003
1848,	87,925		
1849,	67,563		
1850,	64,642		
1851,	72,292	—292,422	73,105
1852,	72,778		
1853,	71,821	—144,599	72,299

XXIX. *Receipts of the Church Missionary Society, England.*

Year.	Receipts.	Periods.	Average Annual Receipts.
1836,	£70,465		
1837,	74,731		
1838,	91,723		
1839,	95,505	—332,424	£83,106
1840,	104,304		
1841,	101,576		
1842,	113,263		
1843,	111,875	—431,018	107,754
1844,	103,661		
1845,	102,495		
1846,	105,059		
1847,	119,410	—430,625	107,456
1848,	115,012		
1849,	101,003		
1850,	94,401		
1851,	101,554	—411,970	102,992
1852,	118,674		
1853,	120,932	—239,606	119,803

Statement concerning a Massachusetts Auxiliary.

There is in Massachusetts an Auxiliary Foreign Missionary Society, [the Brookfield,] embracing at present sixteen churches, which for many years has published an Annual Report, embracing, with but few exceptions, every subscriber's name and the amount of every individual subscription. These Reports furnish statistics of great value. From them, several years ago, tables were constructed, embracing a period of four years, from 1838 to 1841, inclusive; and recently like tables have been made out, embracing four years, from 1847 to 1850, and then also tables comparing the action of the Society for these two periods. The sixteen churches have, in most cases, their own male and female Missionary Associations. They are probably as well organized, as sure to make an annual collection at the proper time, and as sure to do the work well, as any like number of adjoining churches anywhere in the United States.

Summary for the Years 1838–41.

The following table presents a classification of subscriptions, in the years 1838–1841, and shows the number of subscribers under several sums, from six cents up to ten dollars.

Years.	Dollars.						Fractional parts of a dollar.											No. of contributors.	Amount contributed.
	10	5	4	3	2	1	75	60	50	40	37	30	25	20	12	10	6		
1838.																			
Gentlemen, . . .	20	41	2	39	75	279	7	1	153	2	1	2	75		19	5	4	725	$1,184 15
Ladies, ...	4	10	4	21	64	246	27	7	415	6	9	14	441	—	144	30	51	1.493	917 39
	24	51	6	60	139	52[illegible]	34	8	568	8	10	16	516	—	163	35	55	2,218	$2,091 54
1839.																			
Gentlemen, . . .	20	36	4	43	77	283	18		176	1	1	4	126	6	43	5	19	856	1,211 45
Ladies, ...	3	8	5	15	58	264	45	8	450	2	13	11	528	27	140	37	41	1,655	1,019 39
	23	44	9	58	135	547	63	8	626	3	14	15	648	33	183	42	60	2,511	$2,230 84
1840.																			
Gentlemen, . . .	37	29	13	46	98	324	11		225	1	1		137	7	42	18	24	1,013	1,571 13
Ladies, ...		15	8	20	69	281	24	5	478	3	11	11	535	42	161	37	67	1,767	942 64
	37	44	21	66	167	605	35	5	703	4	12	11	672	49	203	55	91	2,780	$2,513 77
1841.																			
Gentlemen, . . .	34	44	11	41	92	267	21	3	184	1	1	6	144		28	6	19	902	1,526 85
Ladies, ...		27	7	19	85	290	54	28	424	8	15	23	556	—	163	49	74	1,822	1,169 37
	34	71	18	60	177	557	75	31	608	9	16	29	700	—	191	55	93	2,724	$2,696 22

General Summary.

Years.	Dollars.						Fractional parts of a dollar.											No. of contributors.	Amount contributed.
	10	5	4	3	2	1	75	60	50	40	37	30	25	20	12	10	6		
1838,	24	51	6	60	139	525	34	8	568	8	10	16	516		163	35	55	2,218	$2,091 54
1839,	23	44	9	58	135	547	63	8	626	3	14	15	618	33	183	42	60	2,511	2,230 84
1840,	37	44	21	66	167	605	35	5	703	4	12	11	672	49	203	55	91	2,780	2,513 77
1841,	34	71	18	60	177	557	75	31	608	9	16	29	700		191	55	93	2,724	2,696 22
	118*	210	54	244	618	2,234	207	52	2,505	24	52	71	2,536	82	740	187	299	10,233	$9,532 37
Aver'e,	29	52	13	61	154	558	51	13	626	6	13	17	634	20	185	46	74	2,558	$2,383 09

* This should be stated $10 and upwards; thirty-five of the subscriptions were over $10.

1838, Contributions at the Monthly Concert, ...	$465 31	
1839, " " " "	647 97	
1840, " " " "	584 45	
1841, " " " "	509 82	
		$2,207 55
Amount of subscriptions, ...		9,532 37
From other sources, ...		276 14
Whole amount of contributions in money, from 1838 to 1841, inclusive, ...		$12,016 06

Summary for the Years 1847–51.

Subscriptions.	No. of Subscribers.	Subscriptions.	No. of Subscribers.
Under 10 cents, ...	333	1 to 2 dollars, ...	151
10 cents, ...	315	2 dollars, ...	484
12½ cents, ...	448	2 to 3 dollars, ...	50
12½ to 25 cents, ...	173	3 dollars, ...	250
25 cents, ...	2,343	3 to 5 dollars, ...	52
25 to 50 cents, ...	133	5 dollars, ...	233
50 cents, ...	2,088	5 to 10 dollars, ...	63
50 to 100 cents, ...	177	10 dollars, ...	113
1 dollar, ...	1,624	Over 10 dollars, ...	83

Whole amount from subscriptions, ...	$10,525 58
From Monthly Concerts and other sources, ...	3,396 40
Total, ...	$13,921 98

Whole amount for four years, including Monthly Concert, . .	$13,921
Average annual amount, ...	$3,480
Number of church members in 1850, ...	2,403
Average annual amount to each, ...	$1 36

Amount raised by the Gentlemen's Associations, ...	$6,027
Average annual amount, ...	$1,506
Male members of the church in 1850, ...	702
Average number of male subscribers, ...	763
Average annual amount to each, ...	$1 96
Average annual amount to each male member of the church, . .	$2 14

Amount raised by Ladies' Associations, ...	$4,208
Average annual amount, ...	$1,052
Female members of the church in 1850, ...	1,701
Average annual number of female subscribers, ...	1,433
Average annual amount to each female subscriber, ...	$0,73
Average annual amount to each member of the church, ...	$0,62

In the "Journal of Missions" for November, 1851, the Rev. Isaac R. Worcester, District Secretary for Massachusetts, remarks as follows, on the statistical tables so usefully printed by the Brookfield Auxiliary.

What do the Statistics published by this Society show?

They show, unexpectedly, that the number of contributors to the American Board in these towns is somewhat smaller now, than it was ten years ago, though nearly the whole amount of falling off is accounted for in a single parish. (The number has diminished in several towns, but in others it has increased) But while the number of subscribers has diminished, the amount subscribed has increased. In the first period the whole amount raised in these towns, including monthly concert contributions, was $11,717 10; in the last period it was $13,921 98, or $3,480 50 annually upon the average. This is about $1 36 to each member of the churches. In the former period the average annual amount was about $1 03 to each church member. One town has increased in its contributions 142 per cent. Another 105 per cent. The increase in the whole Association is about 18½ per cent; though, according to the number of church members, it is 32 per cent. Several churches have fallen off.

The figures show that there are many members of these churches who do nothing for the Board. In fourteen of the churches the number of members in 1850 was 2,403, but the average annual number of subscribers in the last period, in these towns, was but 2,196. Now many subscribe who are not members of the churches. In one parish the number of subscribers is more than twice as great as the number of church members. There must, then, be several hundreds of professing Christians in these churches who do nothing for this Society. How large a part of them contribute to the cause of missions through other channels, we cannot say.

The average annual number of male subscribers, in these 14 towns in the latter period, was 763; 61 more than the number of male members of the churches in 1850. The female members of the same churches in 1850 were 1,701, and the female subscribers in these towns were on the average, only 1,433 annually, for this period; 268 less than the number of female church members. In the former period, the whole average annual number of subscribers in the same 14 towns was 2,353, viz. males, 826; females 1,527; number of church members in 1840, 2,632; males, 815; females, 1,817.

In both periods, therefore, the annual number of male subscribers slightly exceeded the number of male members of the church, while the annual number of female subscribers was considerably less than the number of females in the churches.

The figures show, also, this pleasing fact: that the number of large contributors is increasing. In the former period of four years, there were but thirty-five subscriptions exceeding $10 in amount, and eighty-four of just $10. In the latter period there were eighty three exceeding $10, and one hundred and thirteen of just ten. The number of subscriptions exceeding $2, in the former period, was six hundred and twenty-six; but in the latter it was eight hundred and forty four, though the whole number of subscriptions, as stated above, had diminished. But though the number of large subscriptions has increased, it will be seen that it is still painfully small. Would it have been supposed that for the last four years, in these sixteen towns, there had been but eighty-three subscriptions, (twenty-one annually, upon an average,) out of more than nine thousand in all, exceeding ten dollars?

Again. The figures show that, though some are going forward, a very large part of the subscribers still do but very little. Of 9,113 subscriptions, the whole number in the last period, (omitting some juvenile associations,) 3,612 were in sums not exceeding twenty-five cents each; and 6,010, or 1,502 annually, in sums of less than one dollar each!

The figures show, also, quite too conclusively, that the amount subscribed, generally, is by no means regulated by the exact ability of the subscribers. Subscriptions are in *inconvenient* sums; in sums which constitute a kind of units in our currency. Thus there are 313 subscriptions of ten cents, and 448 of 12½ cents, but only 173 between 12½ and 25 cents, and then 2,343 of 25 cents. There are only 133 between 25 and 50 cents, but 2,088 of 50 cents; 177 all the way between 50 cents and one dollar, and 1,624 of one dollar. From one dollar, the general rule is to go to two, from two to three, from three, not to four, but to five, and from five to ten. Here is a hint for agents and pastors. People need not be urged to *double* their subscriptions, but only to increase. If they increase, they will at least double in a large majority of cases.

Here, too, is a hint for those who sometimes urge a general increase of 12½ per cent., or 25 per cent, upon all subscriptions, to meet the wants of the Board. No such general increase can be secured. The 25 cent subscribers will not go to 28 or 31 cents, nor will the one dollar subscribers often go to 1,12½ or 1,25. Every such effort is vain, in the present state of the church. Men do not calculate so closely upon what they can give. Some of those who give by hundreds and by thousands, may make such a proportionate increase, but not the great number of small contributors.

Much more might be said in regard to what these figures show, but the reader will now be left to his own reflections, with only this additional remark,—they show that even in the best sections of Massachusetts there is much room for improvement. And if this is true of the best sections of this State, what shall be said of the country at large? Can there not be an advance?

RESULTS.

At the meeting of the Board in Troy, N. Y., in 1852, Dr. Anderson, one of the Secretaries, read the following special report, by direction of the Prudential Committee, on the results of the foregoing statistical history of benevolent contributions. It was as follows:

One of the printed documents to be submitted to the Board is a "Statistical History of Benevolent Contributions in the past sixteen years." The immediate occasion of preparing this was, to ascertain why the receipts of the Board have increased no faster during the last ten or twelve years, and what is the prospect in future. This being the object, it was of course necessary to restrict the inquiry to those religious denominations, with which the Board has some immediate connection. The statistical tables are twenty-nine in number, and, though prepared amid numerous cares and interruptions, are believed to be substantially correct. Copies have been distributed among the members; and those who shall give attention to the series of tables, will probably yield their assent to the following results.

1. We divide the receipts of the American Board from 1812 to 1851 into ten periods, of four years each.* There is then found to have been an advance in every period save one, and that was the ninth. That is to say, there was a decline in the receipts of only one period; and there would not have been in that period had it not been for the extraordinary amount of the receipts in 1842, a year belonging to the eighth period. Comparing the experience of the Board with that of the London Missionary Society and of the Church Missionary Society, two of the leading missionary institutions of Great Britain,† we find, though their receipts were considerably larger than ours, that the experience of the Board was more favorable than theirs. The receipts of the London Missionary Society experienced a decline in both of the last two periods of four years, and those of the Church Missionary Society in the last three periods. What the cause of this decline was, has not been investigated, but such was the fact. It is pleasing to be able to add, that the last two years show a rise in the receipts of both those admirable institutions.

2. It is necessary to take several societies into account in reckoning what have been the proper receipts for foreign missions; not only the American Board and the General Assembly's Board of Foreign Missions, but the American Bible Society, the American Tract Society, the American Protestant Society, the Foreign Evangelical Society, the American and Foreign Christian Union, and the American Missionary Association. The Investigation, in respect to most of these societies, is complete only for *the last*

---

* Table i. p. 5.

† Tables xxviii. and xxix. p. 19.

sixteen years, from 1836 to 1851 inclusive; which are divided into four periods of four years each. The grants and payments of the Bible and Tract societies for foreign missions, are reckoned of course as donations. Now it appears in this view, that the receipts for foreign missions of the first period* were $1,204,000, (omitting fractions;) of the second, $1,464,000; of the third, $1,435,000, (there being a small decrease;) and of the fourth $1,763,000. Here is an advance in sixteen years, of pecuniary contributions for foreign missions of $559,000.†

The fact to be especially noted here, is *the wonderful stability of the missionary work*, and *the regularity of its growth.* It should also be observed, that the growth has been very gradual, averaging only about $35,000 a year. One reason for this slow growth may appear as we proceed; but this is the true measure of the growth of the instrumentalities in the work of foreign missions, as carried on by Congregationalists and Presbyterians, through all their organizations; including all they do, and more than all *they* do, for giving the Bible, and religious books and tracts to the papal and heathen world.

3. In four periods out of ten in the Expenditures of the American Board, there was some degree of excess in the expenditure over the receipts; amounting, in forty years, to about $46,000.‡ That account is happily balanced the present year. It also appears,§ that the average annual increase in the cost and expenditure for the missions, during these forty years, has been about $7,000; in the last sixteen years, it was less than five thousand. Now the tables show, that a uniform increase every year is not to be expected. Every society, every good cause, has and will have its fluctuations. In thirteen of the forty-two years ‖ the receipts of the Board were less each year than they were in the year preceding; and the experience of most other societies is similar. It is, therefore, necessary for us to aim at an advance, in the years when an advance is possible, of not less than ten thousand dollars, in order actually to maintain our rate of progress. Yet even such a progress would not admit of our adding as many as ten missionaries, annually, to the number in the field. And should we have that number of missionaries to send, and should we send them, it would be done at the cost of some reduction in our schools, and other auxiliary agencies. *Such, at least, is the result of mere theoretical reasoning*, which many regard as sufficient to govern the proceedings of missionary societies. But experience has thrown new light on this subject. It is now known that there is no real danger of missionary bankruptcy resulting from sending forth well qualified missionaries, who can show reason in their own personal qualities, providential situations, and religious experience, why they ought to go. The missionary work is eminently the Lord's work, based on a special command, a special promise, and a special providence; and it is safe for all to go, whom he calls by his grace and providence to the work; and of course it is safe to send them. It would be safer, in a financial point of view, to send out a score of such men, than to withhold one from fear of the lack of means. The Board tried the policy of withholding men for that reason in the year 1837,—that memorable

* Table xiv. p. 13. † Table xxvii. p. 18. ‡ Table iii. p. 7. § Table ii. p. 6. ‖ Table i. p. 5.

year of ruin in the commercial world,—and has not yet recovered from the paralyzing influence of it on the colleges, theological seminaries and churches. In fact, the only sure way to get the money is, in child-like faith on God, to send forth the men who are called of God to this work. It would seem to be something like a law of the missionary enterprise, that every good missionary shall virtually secure his own support, by the reacting influence of his self-consecration and labors upon the Christian community from which he goes forth. Thus it has been. Every missionary has in fact been supported. Certainly no one from the United States has ever yet been compelled to retire from the field for want of a living. But though missionaries may be expected to have the means of living, if judiciously selected and sent forth, still it is true that their number cannot be increased without a corresponding increase of funds for their support. There is equal truth in both propositions; we must send the men, in order to procure the funds; and there must be the funds, to enable the missionaries to keep the field.

4. Besides nearly four millions of dollars contributed to the American Board during the last sixteen years, there was contributed, in that time,* more than a million of dollars to the General Assembly's Board of Foreign Missions and the American Missionary Association. As this came from churches, most of which, previous to the year 1837, operated through the American Board, a reason is seen why the average annual increase in the receipts of the Board was diminished at the rate of some two thousand dollars. For the actual falling off amounted to no more than a diminution to that extent, in the rate of increase. Supposing this to be one of the principal causes, it ought then to appear that the rate of increase has been better sustained in New England, than it has been elsewhere. And this fact is apparent in the tables.† The increase of donations from New England has been nearly, if not quite, in the ratio of the increased expenditure.

5. Farther light is thrown on the subject, when we look at the progress of the *home missionary enterprise*, during this period.‡ It has been already stated, as a result of these investigations, that the foreign missionary enterprise, in its larger view, has had but a slow increase during the past sixteen years, the average annual rate, within the range of our present inquiries, not having exceeded $35,000. But when we embrace home missions in our view, we see that the *spirit of missions*, the benevolent spirit common to both great branches of the enterprise, has had a somewhat more rapid growth. The general summary view, in the table entitled "Growth of Foreign and Home Missions,"§ shows that in the first period, from 1836 to 1839, the receipts of the foreign and home missions were of almost identically the same amount, the respective sums being $1,204,000, and $1,187,000. But in the last period, from 1848 to 1851, the receipts for home missions exceeded those for foreign missions by $385,000. The sums were $1,763,000, and $2,131,000. The increase of the one had been $559,000, while that of the other was $944,000. An important item of this increase was in the colportage of the Tract Society,‖ which has risen rapidly in favor with the com-

---

* Table xiii. p 13.. † Table vi. pp. 8–10. ‡ Tables xxv. and xxvi. p. 17. § Table xxvii. p. 18. ‖ Table x. p. 12.

munity, the Society having been enabled to expend nearly $450,000 upon it during the ten years past. It is a curious fact, that the *average receipts* of foreign and home missions, for each period of the sixteen past years, is the same within $3,000.* This fact is accounted for by foreign missions having gained considerably on home missions in the second period. It may be interesting to add, that the whole amount of contributions for *foreign* missions, in sixteen years, was $5,868,000, and for *home* missions it was $5,882,000.

6. We see in these Tables how unsatisfactory are the usual comparisons made between the receipts of Foreign and Home Missionary Societies. They are compared as if the receipts of each represented the whole action in the case. But foreign missionary societies do not receive all that is contributed by the Christian community for foreign missions; nor do home missionary societies receive all that is contributed for home missions. Both are directly aided through Bible and Tract Societies; and while all the funds of home missionary societies go for the support of preachers, it inevitably happens, for want of more division and subdivision in the work of foreign missions, that about one-third of the funds of foreign missionary societies are required for schools, the education of native preachers, and the printing of works not embraced in the objects of Bible and Tract Societies. In foreign missions, moreover, what is contributed by native churches toward the support of missionaries, is usually included in the published accounts of the foreign missionary societies, and goes to make up their amount. The course pursued by home missionary societies is deemed a proper one, and is necessarily different. Those generally furnish but a part of the support received by home missionary pastors, (whose relations correspond to those of 'native pastors' in foreign missions,) and what is paid towards their support by the churches to which they minister, is not reckoned among the receipts of home missionary societies, and has no place in our Tables. Besides all this, not only is the work of supplying Bibles and religious books and tracts detached from home missions, (in their restricted, technical sense,) but also colportage, Sabbath schools, theological schools, and indeed every department of education; not to speak of missions in cities.

The only satisfactory comparison, therefore, to be made in the case,—the only one not delusive and injurious to both branches of the great cause,—is a comprehensive one, resembling the one adopted in the construction of these Tables. Such a comprehensive view presents the two in their intimate relations—a vast benevolent association of labors, the glory and blessing of our age.

7. The printed document before us† contains some curious and valuable facts derived from a series of printed annual reports of the Brookfield Auxiliary Foreign Missionary Society in Massachusetts. That Auxiliary contains sixteen churches, each having their own male and female missionary associations, and publishing in their reports, with few exceptions, every subscriber's name and the amount of every individual subscription. From these reports, tables have been made out for two periods of four years each,—from 1838 to 1841, and from 1847 to 1850. The most valuable result

* Table xxvii. p. 18.

† Tables, pp. 20 21.

thus obtained is perhaps what may be called *the law of increase in the matter of benevolent subscriptions.* The results in the second period were as follows:

Subscriptions.	Number of Subscribers.	Subscriptions.	Number of Subscribers.
Under 10 cents,	333	1 to 2 dollars,	151
10 cents,	315	2 dollars,	484
12½ cents,	448	2 to 3 dollars,	50
12½ to 25 cents,	173	3 dollars,	250
25 cents,	2,343	3 to 5 dollars,	52
25 to 50 cents,	133	5 dollars,	233
50 cents,	2,088	5 to 10 dollars,	63
50 to 100 cents,	177	10 dollars,	113
1 dollar,	1,624	Over 10 dollars,	83

The results in the table for the first period, from 1838 to 1841, prepared ten years ago, will be found to correspond remarkably with those just stated as belonging to the second period.

The practical rule to be deduced from this is, that when we exhort the friends of missions to increase their subscriptions, we need not ask them to double, nor to add any certain percentage; but simply *to give more than they have done.* If the exhortation succeeds, and they are left to their own instincts and feelings, they will probably double their subscription, if they have given but twelve and a half, twenty-five or fifty cents, or one dollar, or five dollars. If they have subscribed two dollars, they may subscribe three, or go on to five. If ten, the advance will probably be to fifteen; if fifteen, to twenty or twenty-five; thence on to seventy-five or one hundred. Then the rule goes to two hundred, three hundred, five hundred, a thousand. And when the heart has become so much enlarged, you may expect the advance will be to fifteen hundred, two thousand, five thousand. All of which, as we believe, goes to show, that the great body of contributors do by no means calculate closely as to what they are able to give. A few do, but not the great body. It is chiefly a matter of feeling, convenience, habit, custom,—anything but real ability.

8. The facts embodied in this Statistical History, present to our view the MIGHTY CAUSE OF THE GOSPEL, advancing slowly it is true, but steadily and surely, from year to year, as if borne forward by invincible laws. Nor can we help seeing that the two great branches of the enterprise, besides being most intimately united, do really stimulate and help each other, and that if either one be urged forward, the other will soon move onward by its side. Obviously it is time to give our foreign missions a vigorous setting forward, since they have now fallen somewhat into the rear. This, with God's blessing, will be easily effected, if the pastors of churches, taking courage from the *law of benevolent donations* just stated, shall simply urge their people, now while foreign missions, relieved from embarrassment, are moving steadily upon the track, *to add somewhat* to the little or much they gave the past year in aid of this blessed cause of our Lord and Saviour Jesus Christ.

RESPONSE OF THE BOARD TO THE FOREGOING.

After the reading of this document, it was referred to Henry White, Esq., Rev. Joseph Steele, Dr. Linsley, Horace Holden, Esq., Rev

Isaac R. Worcester, Rev. Ornan Eastman and Rev. Charles H. Reed. This Committee subsequently presented the subjoined report, which was adopted by the Board.

In considering this document your committee have looked at its object, the means by which it has been attempted to attain this object, and the results which are spread out before the Board in the report. The object, as defined in the document, is to ascertain why the receipts of the Board have increased no faster during the last ten or twelve years, and what is the prospect in future. This object needs only to be stated to make its importance and practical bearings felt and acknowledged.

In prosecuting these inquiries, a statistical history of the benevolent contributions of those religious denominations, with which this Board has some immediate connection, has been prepared. This work your committee regard as timely and important. The contributions of these benevolent societies are sufficiently comprehensive, both in extent of territory and of time, to be made legitimately the basis of the calculations of the science of statistics,—that wonderful science of these latter days, which, out of facts the most uncertain and variable, deduces principles and conclusions the most certain and unchanging. It is important to be in possession of all the light which such investigations afford; and the present position of the Board, as free from debt and yet not advancing in its receipts at the rate at which it once did, renders the investigation timely.

These inquiries, so important and timely, necessarily involve a comparison of the receipts of different departments of the great missionary work; and, indeed, thinking minds will be unavoidably led by such statistics to such comparisons. The printed document accompanying the report, does not profess to have attained entire accuracy, but offers itself as containing suggestions of some of the principles which should guide in such comparisons. Your committee, in the short time alloted to them, are not prepared to say that improvements may not be made in the arrangement which the printed document makes of the various societies, under the two great heads of the foreign missionary work and home missionary work. That for the purposes of a true comparison, some such comprehensive classification, as is there attempted, should be made, seems to the committee obvious. Neither are the committee, on the other hand, prepared to say that the classification made is not correct. There are some societies, such as the Education Society, in regard to the proper position of which, whether as wholly a home work, or in part a preparation for foreign work, minds may be expected to differ; and in regard to which, if a classification of their receipts is attempted, there would be great difficulty in finding the proper rule for such a division. If the results of this attempt should make a further prosecution of these inquiries desirable, the principles which should guide in such a classification, could be carefully reviewed, and more fully stated.

Your committee have been greatly interested in the results of these inquiries, as drawn out at length in the report referred to them. It is delightful and encouraging to find, as a sure conclusion, drawn from unquestionable data, that the mighty cause of the gospel is advancing steadily and surely. Your committee are confident that the two great branches of the gospel work, at home and abroad, are so intimately blended, that the progress of the one is sure in the end to secure also that of the other. Fluctuations in progress have been experienced, and are to be expected; yet these fluctuations should not discourage us. The statistics presented show that the great cause is onward. The contributions to the different American societies, here brought to view, were about $1,500,000 more during the four years ending in 1851, than they were during four years ending in 1839. This is an increase of about sixty-three per cent. upon the receipts of the former period, or in twelve years. At this rate of increase the contributions of our churches to benevolent objects will double in less than twenty years. With reference to the single period of four years in which there was a decline in the receipts of this Board, the statistics make it very obvious, that there was not a decline on the whole in the benevolent efforts of the churches. During that period the receipts of the American Bible Society, of the American Tract Society, and of the American Home Missionary Society, increased greatly; these three societies together having received in that time about $271,000 more than during the previous four years. Benevolent contributions were then increasing; and it is believed that Christians were not coming to love the cause of foreign missions less, but, for many reasons, were coming to feel a deeper interest in various efforts for the good of our own land.

But while God permits us, for the strengthening of our faith, to see at intervals, as it were, that the movement of his chariot wheels is onward, yet your committee would not forget that such cheering views, vouchsafed for our refreshment, are not to be made indispensable to our efforts, or the measure of them. We have been led, during this meeting of the Board, to dwell much on the leading rule and motive for our missionary labors. We are to walk in this work by faith, and not by sight. In the language of the report under consideration, it is the Lord's work, based on a special command, a special promise, a special providence. We must labor, therefore, each in his lot, and with the abilities of which he has made us the stewards.

And in connection with this thought, your committee would call attention to the result of Christian experience alluded to in the report, as throwing light upon and modifying the results of our theoretical reasoning; namely, that there is no real danger of embarrassment resulting from sending forth well qualified missionaries, who can show reason in their own personal qualities, providential situations, and religious experience, why they ought to go. It is safe for them to go; it is safe to send them. Still it remains true, as the report suggests, that the number of such missionaries cannot be increased without a corresponding increase of funds for their support.

The statements of these statistical tables show us that the foreign missionary work is not advancing as rapidly as it should. It is timely then to urge, as the report does, that we should now give to our foreign missions a vigorous setting forward. And while the curious and interesting statistics of the Brookfield auxiliary, so minutely detailed in the report, give us some light as to the manner in which the call upon the churches can best be made, there can be no doubt that it is highly important and necessary, that all the members of our churches should now be urged to add to that which they have heretofore been accustomed to give, that this department of the Lord's work may not suffer.

www.ingramcontent.com/pod-product-compliance
Lightning Source LLC
LaVergne TN
LVHW011136110826
845150LV00008B/2375
9781418194512